J. Watson

The Secret Disciple

Encouraged to Avow his Master

J. Watson

The Secret Disciple

Encouraged to Avow his Master

ISBN/EAN: 9783337395490

Printed in Europe, USA, Canada, Australia, Japan

Cover: Foto ©Lupo / pixelio.de

More available books at **www.hansebooks.com**

THE SECRET DISCIPLE

ENCOURAGED

TO AVOW HIS MASTER.

BY THE LATE
REV. J. WATSON.

"What concord hath Christ with Belial?"—PAUL.

New Edition.

London:
HODDER AND STOUGHTON,
27, PATERNOSTER ROW.

TO THE READER.

THIS little book, which has passed through three Editions, is now re-issued, with the hope that it may answer the end for which it was originally designed by the author, whose signally useful career was so suddenly terminated some years ago by a most melancholy accident, still fresh in the memory of many; and be of service to a large and interesting class of individuals, who, though they belong to the flock of Christ, often live and die at a distance from His fold.

CONTENTS.

	PAGE
INTRODUCTION	9
CHAP. I.—PLEAS EXAMINED	11
CHAP. II.—REASONS WHY ALL WHO LOVE JESUS CHRIST SHOULD AVOW HIM BEFORE MEN	39

INTRODUCTION.

THE SECRET DISCIPLE DESCRIBED.

THERE are, in almost all religious denominations, many persons who attend the services of the sanctuary, and engage in the exercises of devotion, without making a profession of Christianity. Like Joseph of Arimathea, they are "disciples of Jesus," but it is "secretly." The excellences they possess are not known to be the offspring of piety. Their convictions are deep and frequent, though indicated too obscurely to strike common apprehension. In retirement the Bible is their companion, and in public it is "the man of their counsel," save that no one is aware of the authority they acknowledge. Conscious of their need of pardon and moral renovation, they have "fled for refuge to the hope set before them in the gospel," and are seeking by faith and prayer those heavenly influences which God has promised to the Church. Yet these inward struggles are so hidden by a show of worldly compliance, by no distinct avowal of attachment to the Saviour, by unbroken reserve on religious topics, and nothing more than mute, emphatic attention to direct personal appeal, that the *fact* has transpired only in subsequent confession, perhaps in the near prospect of eternity. A young man who was visited by a friend of the writer some time ago, exactly answered this description. During the progress of pulmonary consumption, to which he at last fell a victim, he listened most attentively to "the truth as it is in Jesus," but said scarcely anything, and was not known to possess a copy of the sacred volume, until he chanced to be found reading it in a lonely walk, a little before his dissolution. He then owned the interest he felt in the gospel, the comfort he drew from the promises of God, and his unshaken hope of immortality. Up to that moment his heart had been a dark recess, no one had explored its secrets, and he threw it open only just as the flickering taper of life betokened its speedy extinction. The position of such an individual is singular and inconsistent. Renouncing the principles of the world, he is one with it in appearance; and embracing the principles of the Church, he yet remains totally alienated from her communion. Knowing that instances of a like kind are by no means rare, the object of this little work is to examine a few of the pleas which are urged for this secrecy, with the view of encouraging a public confession of the name of Christ.

THE SECRET DISCIPLE

Encouraged to Avow his Master.

---o---

CHAPTER I.

PLEAS EXAMINED.

1. *Fear of opposition, persecution, losses, etc.*—It is a general truth, that "godliness is profitable unto all things," though as to "the promise of the life that *now* is," it admits of exceptions, unless we throw into the scale the pure satisfaction of goodness as an ample equivalent for privations of other kinds. Still man is the creature of various affections, which have their own ends, and are not to be appeased with the proper aliment of conscience—the pleasure of uprightness. If a sense of rectitude could meet their demands, if we could pacify hunger by recollecting the truth of our opinions and the justice of our cause, we could bid defiance to nature, say farewell to trial, and trample on the world. In this case, however, we should not have those tests of principle which both manifest its existence and prove its weakness or its power. Thus we see that fear of the Jews—the fear of

being put out of the synagogue, and bearing the infamy of excommunication—worked on the mind of Joseph, and induced him to conceal his real sentiments with respect to the Messiah. And though *we* have not to make the extensive sacrifices which were common in the apostolic age, many Christians, especially in the earlier indications of religious feeling, have to encounter no small share of persecution. A man's foes are they of his own household; and occasionally they rise against him abroad as well as at home, employing every form of ridicule, meanness, and malice, in order to shake the purpose of his soul. It often, however, happens, that these apprehensions are fallacious, and are indulged on no good foundation. But even admitting the worst, it can in no sense justify secrecy and indecision. The fear of man, in matters of religion, must ever be an unworthy principle of action. It is not necessary to define the limits within which this motive may be allowed a subordinate post in watching over our interests, but we may remark that it never adds dignity to character, and in the question before us is manifestly improper. By allowing it to operate, we place a fellow-creature above the Deity. One would imagine that no second thought was needed to frown it down for ever. We may in this respect take a lesson from those who are not only "wiser," but bolder "in their generation than the children of light." Men of science, in the present age, would be ashamed of that pusillanimity which would attend to a tyrant's threat, and conceal the phenomena of nature. They would either endure the penalties of disclosure, or sacrifice the associations of country and home, to pursue elsewhere their favourite investigations. They would seek truth in a pure and open element, where she might "live, move, and have her being," in any and every shape, without molestation. Could this asylum not be found, they would, at last, sacrifice themselves on her altars.

Perhaps, however, we are not to expect men to act thus boldly in the avowal of religious convictions. But why not? Is religion less sacred than science? Are its truths less important? Is the homage due to conscience less than is due to the depraved antipathies of a sinner at enmity with God? Only one answer can be given to these questions. No silence on abstract or political truth, within the hearing of despotic ignorance, can be so ignoble as silence on topics of immortal interest, if forced by the pressure or power of any human being. On entering the society of such persons, one must reflect somewhat as follows :—

" Here I must not speak or act as if I believed in the existence, benevolence, and providence of God. I must avoid all expressions of admiration at His constant bounty, and take special care never to name the incarnation and sufferings of Christ as the basis of all my hopes of pardon and acceptance hereafter. Any serious allusion to the corruption of the heart, the influences of the Holy Spirit, the doctrines of faith and regeneration, will be an unpardonable offence. All the solemn views I entertain of heaven and hell, guilt and reconciliation, are never to appear in discourse, but to suffer an oblivion as effectual as if they had no existence. A few worldly maxims and concessions will make my friends think well of me, as not irrecoverably gone. A gleam of hope will cross their minds, that I may yet disappoint the godly, and swell the triumphs of impiety. This will make for my comfort in present circumstances, while a contrary course, a fixed resolution to serve God, will render my days miserable and realize my worst apprehensions. I must then put up with a cold, unsympathising intercourse, instead of the happiness and animation of social life, where all is cordiality and love." *

* In Ireland this is often the case, especially with those females who embrace Protestantism. Unjust duties are im-

It is not seldom that thoughts of this cast get the better of conviction. All that is pure in conception, deep in feeling, and, from its connection with human character and hopes, invested with unutterable interest, is thus entombed at once. The temple of God is stripped to propitiate a foe. An impending ill is magnified out of due proportion, so as to exclude from view what is infinitely more awful. Haunted by the spectre of present evils,—vexation, malicious treatment, misrepresentation, etc., the individual forgets that darker terrors will gather over futurity, on the recollection that *duty* was abandoned at the bidding of a shadow, and that the menacing attitude of depravity did more to decide the mind than the known, certain, complacent approval of all existing uprightness. When conscience shall fully awake, this will be no grateful reminiscence, but more like the morning watch, when God looked through the pillar of fire and cloud upon the host of the Egyptians. It will seem to the sinner's feelings as if the Almighty were his foe, that he may grow fully sensible of posed, which must be discharged meekly, unless they are prepared to bear the peevishness of a whole family. I have known cases in which the joy of home has been lost by a change of opinion, and in the room of maternal and sisterly affection, a violent antipathy has displayed itself in unrelenting persecution.

the difference there is between the scorn that plays on the lips, or the scowl that settles on the brow of the workers of iniquity, and the appalling, righteous displeasure of the Supreme Judge. There is force in these considerations, even supposing individuals secure present comfort by a guilty suppression of the truth. It often, however, happens that God mars at once all their plans of pacification "They have put themselves to pain, but shall not profit," is a decision to which He gives immediate effect. He "disannuls their covenant with hell," and instantly their hopes vanish, like the fitful, momentary light that plays upon the clouds: "Because thou hast forgotten the God of thy salvation, and hast not been mindful of the Rock of thy strength, therefore shalt thou plant pleasant plants, and shalt set it with strange slips: in the day shalt thou make thy plant to grow, and in the morning shalt thou make thy seed to flourish: but the harvest shall be a heap in the day of grief and of desperate sorrow."

As this motive, the fear of a fellow-mortal, is unworthy of a disciple of Christ, the Saviour has placed it under most emphatic prohibition. He has threatened to disown before His Father those who are ashamed of Him or of His words. Selecting the last calamity that man can inflict on man, He thus addresses Himself to us : "I say unto you, my friends, Be not afraid of them that kill the body, and after that have no more that they can do. But I will forewarn you whom ye shall fear : Fear Him, who, after He hath killed, hath power to cast into hell ; yea, I say unto you, Fear Him."

2. *Fear of dishonouring the Christian profession.*—That the reason here assigned for secresy in religion operates extensively, is evident from the acknowledgments of numbers who at length approach the table of the Lord. When urged to adopt a decided course, they have either changed or evaded the topic of conversation, owing to the apprehension of some future fall. The nature of this plea demands considerable indulgence. When perfectly sincere, it is one of the most amiable excuses that can be given for not pledging heart and soul to the Church of Christ. There may be that tender regard to His honour which would dread even " the appearance of evil." And under the impression that it is possible not only to *err*, but to *sin*, the best and most conscientious of mankind may be kept from identifying themselves with the solemn obligations of the Christian profession. These, however, are the very individuals about whom all who are anxious for the

prosperity of Zion should feel the greatest interest, encouraging them, whether old or young, "to subscribe with their hand unto the Lord." "The feeling you have," one might say, "proves your concern for the glory of God, though it is at variance with immediate duty." There would be some good reason for hesitation if you were sent this warfare "at your own charges." As it is, the command of Christ to confess Him before men, to come out from the world, and to commemorate His love, is binding on all His followers; and the promise of Christ, "My grace is sufficient for you," is so animating that you have only to consider and to plead it in order to a new state of feeling—as if the Great Head of the Church had lent His hand to establish your goings. The *fear* you entertain may even be salutary. A traveller who questions the soundness of his path will be guarded in his steps; and a sense of moral feebleness and exposure may be of use to remind you of Him who can help you in adversity—knowing, as He does, all the dangers of the way, and being ever able and willing to afford protection.

Suppose, now, we venture a step farther, and put the case that you do *not* "adorn the doctrine of God your Saviour in all things," are you there-

Encouraged to Avow his Master. 19

fore to renounce your Sovereign because, on some occasions, you may be guilty of disaffection? Are you to allow the open ravages of an enemy in a territory under your care, because you fear that now and then he will obtain a triumph? Perhaps the remote thought of imitating the treachery of Peter would silence you for life; you would not deny your Master for the world. It is well to stand in awe of sin, and far be it from me to blunt the sensibility of the heart toward God; but apart from every such thought, there is yet room for the question—" Had Peter never avowedly followed Christ, never denied him, except *always*, never had to repent but on a death-bed, would it have been well or ill for the Church and the world?" Who would have hesitated, had it been proposed either not to have the apostle at all, or to have him as he was—an average specimen of human nature? There can be no doubt that his fall did him good, and many others can testify the happy effect of their infirmities in humbling them before God, when they stood high in the estimation of men. So that allowing it possible that you may not exemplify the gospel to perfection, or that you may in some instances dishonour it, it does not follow, on any great scale, that this shall be a calamity to mankind.

It will try the honesty of some who are glad to find a stumbling-block in their way to furnish them with a pretext for going out of it. *That's religion!* will be their calumnious exclamation, when you disgrace your cause, should it be matter of private tattle or of public notoriety. Few will show you pity, or intercede for you at the throne of mercy. Your own feelings will be indescribable. Truth, gratitude, consistency, purity, will all make their appeal to conscience, and fill you with pangs of remorse. All the sorrows you have ever known of another kind, will appear light and lenient compared with this, though it have in the end a beneficial influence on Christian character. Genuine repentance induces carefulness, zeal, and a double improvement of the energy that remains to make up for past negligence. One who had traced this path in its sins and its sorrows, used to say, "The Church is right: I am justly doomed to *go softly all my days in the bitterness of my soul*, but there is still scope for doing good where my faults are unknown, and there will I distribute tracts, or exert myself in other ways, and thus *avenge myself upon the devil!*" Think not, my friend, that I would palliate evil—it is "a deadly poison." But the injunction of the blessed Saviour is imperative as to your present duty, and my sole aim is to show, that if you should *not* invariably fight "as a good soldier of Jesus Christ," it is not a legitimate consequence, as your backwardness would insinuate, that you are never to draw the sword out of its scabbard, never to "come to the help of the Lord, to the help of the Lord against the mighty."

Thus would I address a disciple of Christ under the fear of religious declension. It is true that he has nothing to do with the future; his only care should be to "watch and pray," and therefore the reasonings we adopt with any individual of this class should not be allowed to obscure the higher principles of moral obligation. It will be, however, his own fault, if, in the present case, he do not distinguish between what is submitted to him, *granting* his consequences, and what is urged upon him as instant *duty*, apart from all possible events. The latter is the only consideration that will bear the light of the last day. Futurity is the province of Omniscience. The habit of acting on the will of God the moment that we know it, is incumbent on us as accountable creatures: "Speak unto the children of Israel that they go forward." Whenever we listen to the Divine command, the Angel of the covenant will go before us to point out the way to the land of promise. The temptations that are common to man may assail us; but "neither death, nor life, nor angels (demons), nor principalities, nor powers, nor things present, nor things to come, nor height, nor depth, nor any other creature shall be able to separate us from the love of God, which is in Christ Jesus our Lord."

3. *The inconsistency of professing Christians.*— When it happens that a minister or friend is admitted to the religious secrets of another's breast, and advises a public recognition of the claims of Christ, he is often met by a reply of this kind,— "Why, I don't know whether to do so or not; there is so much profession, and so little practice, that I am at a loss how to account for it, and think it almost if not quite as well to remain as I am."

There need be no hesitation in allowing the partial truth of this charge, though, if intended to apply to all Christian societies, it is uncharitable and false. *Consistent* professors make up the majority of our Churches. In general it may be said that their domestic deportment, and their public character and exertions involve, almost necessarily, a systematic attack on all the vices. Men are inconsistent in particular acts, as were Abraham, Isaac, and Jacob, but as a whole they exemplify their real principles. Cases of absolute hypocrisy are not contemplated in the objection, and, if they are, they ought not to be, since such cases attest the value and loveliness of religion. When Satan transforms himself into an angel of light, he owns the power of virtue, and does unwilling homage to a superior nature. There are spots in the sun. No community is exempt from defects; but they are, for the most part, such as we might anticipate from the condition of human nature. Deviations from the spirit of the gospel often occur, which it is impossible to bring under the operation of ecclesiastical discipline. They can be met only by private remonstrance, or by the persuasive force of truth in its public ministration. Imperfections occasionally make their appearance in nine-tenths of our communicants, and we often judge of the entire character from a single act of impropriety. In some cases this is necessary on account of the contagion of bad example. We may, however, lay it down as a rule, that the greatest tenderness is to be shown to the followers of Christ that is compatible with the ends of their association. It is easy to discriminate where an exception should be made to stand the censure of the Church. As to the general question, were any other than overt acts to guide the judgment of Christian societies, their own existence would instantly be endangered. A prying and censorious spirit would take the place of the charity that "bears with the infirmities of the weak;" and the self-distrust that considers its own liability to temptation would be exchanged for a stoical severity that would restore no brother who had been once "overtaken in a fault." We advocate not licence; we only inculcate "the meekness and gentleness of Christ" towards "men of like passions with ourselves." We may give an instance for illustration. The persons who withhold their sanction from the Christian Church on the ground of its defective membership, *may*, some time or other, need an ingenuous and tender construction of their own conduct. They must be singularly free from mistakes and foibles if they never call for the clemency of their fellow-creatures. Let their rule then be applied at home. Can they expect the mercy they have not shown? Will not the feelings of mankind authenticate the retributory maxim, "With what measure ye mete it shall be measured to you again?" Assuredly they will. A hard heart chills the sympathies of nature, while the man who confesses an error of temper, appetite, or conduct, is regarded with tenfold pity, when we know that his own breast is filled with the love that "covers a multitude of sins."

We therefore address to such persons this alternative :—If the defects you condemn be sufficiently aggravated for ecclesiastical discipline, you should be where you may give your vote for that corrective measure which they demand. If they be *not* thus guilty and affecting, if they do *not* touch the vitals of personal Christianity, you carry your scruples to an uncharitable length. Such offences are incident to humanity. Disunity on these grounds can never be justified at the bar of Scripture. *It* enjoins us to consider ourselves lest we also be tempted—an exercise always becoming sinful creatures, and never to be forgotten in our judgments of human conduct. Should you ever sit down at the Lord's table on earth, you must sit down with imperfection. A credible profession—a profession that indicates sincerity of mind, repentance towards God, and faith in the Lord Jesus Christ—is the only qualification essential to the communion of saints. Where this is found, minor faults may be amended by the exhibition of a higher character. Fix on this post for yourself. You will do it honour if you are what you ought to be—superior to the censures you inflict. You will raise the temperature of piety by your warmth : you will shed around you an influence that will be felt by many while you know it not, and the grace of the Spirit, adorning your whole life, will make you a light to the Church and to the world.

4. *Doubtfulness of their own state.*—It is matter of great anxiety with some persons to know whether or not they really have passed from death unto life. They do not like to venture within the pale of the Church till they are satisfied of their own piety. They require personal assurance. Others, who are admitted to their confidence, see in them unquestionable tokens of the great change. Their views of the Saviour and of themselves, of the doctrines and of the precepts of the gospel, are indicative of "a new heart and a right spirit." But because their experience comes short of that which is the fruit of more mature judgment and meditation, they conclude that they have "neither part nor lot in the matter." Now all this arises from the supposition of *a fixed standard of religious emotion.* But no such thing exists. The mind is subject to as many modifications as the atmosphere. We rise from calmness to intensity. When Peter met the eye of his Master, he "went out and wept *bitterly ;*" a state of feeling which required not

only his original susceptibility, but all the attendant aggravations of his sin.

Though, however, each case may present some peculiarity, the fact of a taste for moral purity is as discoverable by consciousness as a taste for music. Suppose the question to be, whether or not you love truth? The appeal must be made to facts and to your feelings. Personal advantage has never induced you to depart from it, nor for the sake of saving appearances have you ever resorted to equivocation. You hate duplicity— you are conscious of this—that is, you love ingenuousness and truth with all your heart.

At this point pause, and let the inquiry be, whether or not you love Jesus Christ? A similar process of thought will go far to settle the question. Fathom your own consciousness. As you are a *secret* disciple there are only a few who form a correct apprehension of you, though the scanty and scattered *data* on which they judge are favourable to your character. This may be presumptive evidence of something in you not absolutely hostile to religion, and possibly you may find it confirmed on an appeal to your inmost soul. Perhaps, then, you are *sure* you have no such feeling towards the truth, purity, self-denial, and benevolence of the blessed Jesus as you have towards he base artifices of the hypocrite. On the contrary, you yield Him the unfeigned homage of your heart, and bend before Him as the great exemplar of all goodness. As such you read the narrative of His life, and pray for a like mind, while dwelling on His love, and musing amidst the wonders of the Cross. You plead His name for the pardon of sin, which shows that you think it has a virtue peculiar to itself, not to be found in any "other name under heaven given among men." Perhaps, also, you confide in Christ as *sensibly* as you believe in the existence of God or a future state. If you question, therefore, your faith in the merits of the one, to be consistent you ought to question your faith in the being of the other: that is, whether in truth you are not an atheist.

As this is by no means likely, the probability of your disbelief of Christian verities, and dislike of Christian virtues, receives on the same grounds a similar diminution. Ascertain the facts of the case. Examine your affections. Love, admiration, trust, spirituality, etc., are all intimated to others by outward acts, by inward tendencies and operations to ourselves.

But you will, it may be, say, "I do not think that my heart could be so hard, so indifferent to private devotion, so little moved at the love of Christ, if I really belong to Him. I see a difference in other persons, and indubitable evidence of their union with the Great Head of the Church."

Now, however much your apathy is to be deplored, this is recurring to the old position of some fixed standard of devotional sentiment. You do not doubt whether you are alive because others have a greater measure of vital energy. The sap of one tree shoots up rapidly, another is slow in its growth; they have life in various degrees. Such men as Brainerd and Payson—men of pre-eminent piety—complained of not being affected, as were some of their brethren, with "the great things of God." These are painful lamentations, taking their rise in what is true, but often clogged with consequences that are false. A feeble pulsation indicates life, though it is expedient that the subject of this weakness should listen to every suggestion which may tend to improve the tone of the system, and give him a vigorous circulation. Not to urge that solicitude is itself a proof of attachment to the Saviour, it is obvious that you are examining the question by an improper standard—the attainments of other Christians—not the *nature* of your own affections, and their accordance with the spirit and principles of the gospel.

It is not conclusive for you to say, "Paul *knew* in whom he believed, and was blessed with the full assurance of faith; *therefore*, if I were a Christian, my experience would be like his." What man disclaims his kind, because he has not the strength of Samson? A twig, that bends in the breeze, is often of the same species as the tree that swings its mighty arms amidst the whirlwind.

Moral character, springing from the most exalted source, one in origin and end, yet exists in all varieties of strength. Provision is therefore made in the Church of Christ for receiving all shades of discipleship, from the twilight of Christian knowledge to perfect day. The Saviour, in fact, laid down this comprehensive principle: "He that is not against us is on our side." In spiritual growth we fall in with the analogies of nature, and put out "first the blade, then the ear, after that the full corn in the ear."

It will hence appear that the question you have to settle is not one of *degrees*, but of *kind*. You justly conclude your tastes to be like those of other human beings if you have one common object in pursuit. Now, good men, good books, good principles, meet in you the most cordial approbation. You have an affection for them. Their contraries, according to the degree of corruption, you view with totally other emotions, from simple displacency to utter abhorrence. The love of God, the character, doctrines, and institutions of Christ, the office and influences of the Spirit, are subjects far more congenial to your mind than those which involve the extinction of piety, and a willing, wanton forgetfulness of the claims and discoveries of revelation. In fine, you would rather come to the light, and render your deeds manifest, than escape from it to wrap yourselves up in darkness. You are more disposed to sit under the word, to learn the plague of your own heart, than to administer an opiate to conscience by plunging into the vanities of life.

These, then, we say, are the seeds of good things. They ascertain the actual existence of the religious affections. Though at present in their infancy, proper aliment will nurture them up into manhood. This will be found in the means of grace. Obedience to the will of God, and an attendance on the ordinances of Christ, act like the warmth and light and showers of heaven, in quickening and invigorating plants of righteousness: "They that wait upon the Lord shall renew their strength; they shall mount up with wings as eagles; they shall run, and not be weary; and they shall walk, and not faint."

5. *Secret piety sufficient.*—Some persons have been known to justify the reserve we treat of, by quoting certain texts of Scripture, which inculcate the religion of the heart. "Jesus Christ," say they, "teaches us to pray to our Father in *secret*. He attended at the temple, and thus encouraged public instruction, but privately He admonished His disciples to cherish that hidden goodness which shuns the common gaze of mankind. Even almsgiving and fasting were to be practised without allowing others to know either our piety or devotion. This is the way to keep the spring of virtue pure, when, like Bethesda, it is moved only by an unseen power, and imparts its salutary properties to numbers who cannot explore the source whence they flow. The public atmosphere is foul, it affects our motives the instant we breathe it, and taints all actions of the best kind, since they then must of necessity transpire in a crowd. At least, therefore, *we* may be permitted to remain among the *hidden ones*, when so many are forward to avow their principles." This plea is founded on a misapprehension of the scope and purpose of our Lord's teaching. The principal Pharisees were plausible hypocrites, who turned the outward acts and symbols of religion, prayer, donations, etc., into instruments of avarice and wickedness. They

were devout everywhere but at home. All their sanctity was a disguise, beneath which the eye of Omniscience saw only the grossest forms of corruption. It is against this leaven the disciples are cautioned: "God is a Spirit, and they that worship Him must worship Him in spirit and in truth." A *hollow* profession is an abomination to the Searcher of hearts. Here the prohibition applies. Sincerity, benevolence, grace, were to fill the void, and to render the air and language of devotion expressive of the various qualities of Christian excellence. The Saviour said in effect, " Religion with you, my followers, is not to be a mere shadow, but a great and solemn reality."

All this, however, contains no allusion to the external structure of the Church. The question is not mooted whether the invisible things of the kingdom of God shall or shall not have any visible indication. This had been settled virtually by the disciples taking up their cross and following Christ. *They* were not a secret society. The commands of their Master imposed publicity on them. The institution of the Lord's Supper was a direct measure to this end, necessarily including, even if celebrated with closed doors, fraternal association. Hence we are told that the primitive Christians, "met together on the first day of the week to break bread."

All who joined them adopted the usual practice, as the only clear meaning of the injunction, "Do this in remembrance of me." We are to follow in the same path. This ordinance is the symbol of spiritual life, as well as the most affecting memento of the Saviour's love. No occasion is more impressive, none more calculated to perpetuate the unity of the Spirit in the bond of peace. Then it is, when mingling hopes and fears, petitions and thanksgivings at the cross, that his followers realize, more than at any other time, the true communion of saints.

Prophecy tells us, that "the mountain of the Lord's house shall be exalted above the hills, and that all nations shall flow unto it." The co-operation of believers of every name, either in local societies for spiritual purposes, or in those great institutions which collect and marshal the forces of "the Prince of peace," to reduce the whole earth to the obedience of faith, is the fulfilment of this prediction. Isaiah had an ideal representation, filled with grand though it may be vague conceptions of our present state, when he was aiming to descry and foretell the glory of the Church. Scenes of this kind relieve the dark map of human nature. They spread light and beauty over large spots of the globe, which would otherwise be lost in "the valley of the shadow of death." But it is proper to remind the reader that while the isles and continents of Christendom attest the faithfulness of God, they do so by the outward and visible signs of the Christian profession. Let this be abandoned, let the disciples of the Lord Jesus come to Him, only " by night," only when screened from human observation, and this standing proof of the Divine veracity will be lost to the world.

The Saviour may deal tenderly with such minds as wait on Him in secret to listen to His voice, and to do homage at His feet, but He will soon apprize them of the cross they have to bear, and that it is good for them to bear it even in their youth. It is impossible to examine His will with a sincere intention to obey it, and yet remain neutral and disguised in a conflict in which He "musters the hosts to the battle." While the painful process of "halting between two opinions" is going on, conscience, as the advocate of His claims, will reiterate her demand for the open avowal of His name. The peace which the soul enjoys in a cheerful compliance with all the requisitions of Scripture will not bless their solitude. A sense of indecision, of essential defectiveness in attachment to the cause of Christ, will embitter their meditations. All those thoughts which, like ministering spirits, dwell in the hearts and sweeten the sorrows of the just, will merely light on the mind, and finding their purpose marred by weak pretences, will take flight, and return to their own place, instead of resting, as did the dove on the head of the Saviour, in complacent association with Christian manliness, obedience, and love. A voice like that which came to the prophet in the cave—"What dost thou here?" will haunt every secret disciple until, throwing off his mask, he show his true features, and be at once disowned by the world, and welcomed by the Church into the fellowship of the sons of God.

Our object, it will be observed, is not to say anything respecting the *final* happiness of this class, though we doubt not that the present will, in some way or other, impress itself on the future, as "with the pen of iron, and the point of a diamond." Admitting, however, their safety, will they be satisfied with this? We trust not. The character of the blessed and only Potentate requires vindication; a palpable exhibition of the gospel is a duty which none can neglect without guilt; the disciples of Christ are to sound the trumpet, which is to awaken the slumbers of mankind; believers are to be one family, "one body," "members one of another;" and in no light, humanly speaking, can the purposes of Heaven come to pass but by the direct junction and array of all who are on the Lord's side against the enemies of truth. Hence it will appear, that to insinuate the sufficiency of secret piety is to overlook all the *social* ends of the Christian vocation. It is to allege as the will of God that which negatives His will, and to gratify a false delicacy by setting aside the claims of man, the commands of Christ, and the authority of revelation. With the heart we are to believe, with the mouth to make confession, and whoever shrinks from the latter, under any circumstances, casts a doubt upon his faith, and brings a cloud upon his soul. The Sun of righteousness never riseth on the path of disobedience and sin : that, on the contrary, which displays a reverential regard to the laws of Christ, though occasionally overcast, is the native track on which He sheds a mild and cheering radiance to a thousand generations.

Whether, therefore, the foregoing or other reasons be assigned for delaying an open rupture with the enemies of Christ, they must all fall under condemnation. The best of them is bad. The fear of disgracing the Christian cause looks as well as any excuse in this matter can look ; yet if we reduce it to its first principles, either there is no such thing as moral evil, or it means this—a fear lest the individual should sometimes find himself fully disposed to become a worker of iniquity. If there be little apprehension of glaring crime, and hesitation rest on negative grounds, the fear of not honouring the Saviour, rather than of positively dishonouring Him, it will amount to the same thing—a kind of assurance that the individual will not, at all times, be inclined to cultivate the graces of the Spirit, and to live by faith on the Lord Jesus Christ. But these are voluntary, controllable, and therefore culpable states of mind. They need not be indulged, and apart from the will they never can exist. Hence it follows, that, in the question before us, a possible future determination of a moral agent to act as he ought not is made the reason of a present determination to act in the same way. Whoever, in things of this nature, *makes* must *unmake*, or stand guilty before God. It is the prerogative of a rational being to review, modify, and change his principles of action. The sternest necessitarians use language sufficiently concessive for the purpose of this argument. " Counsels are the causes of effects. We are moved to prayer by outward objects, as pious company, godly preachers, or something equivalent." *

* Hobbes. Tripos. pp. 291, 303, 12mo. 1684.

Hoping to produce some "effect" on the hearts of secret disciples, we submit to them the following additional considerations. May the Spirit of God invest them with power equal to their right! Should it please Him so to do, numbers, who now are silent and fearful followers of Christ, will henceforth boldly encounter the perils of their way, will deem it their joy and crown to confess His name, and will no longer sacrifice conscience to expediency, or the authority of God to the usurpations of the flesh.

CHAPTER II.

REASONS WHY ALL WHO LOVE JESUS CHRIST SHOULD AVOW HIM BEFORE MEN.

1. *Christianity has made no provision for secret discipleship.*—In some ancient schools of heathen philosophy it was usual to have two classes of pupils, one to which truth was presented in a disguised and popular form, while to the other she was introduced without a veil, after its members had been fitted to contemplate her genuine, unmasked features by a peculiar initiation. Though pagan nations treated with unpardonable neglect "the things that are made"—the chief medium

they had of arriving at correct apprehensions of the eternal Power and Godhead—they still were sensible, to a certain extent, that the Deity is other than matter—an incorporeal and perfect intelligence. There were many important truths relative to the government, character, and providence of God, at which we find a momentary glance, intimating the existence of light, which, though faint at the best, was yet not fed and followed, till it should shed around a purer and wider illumination. This was the case at least as to public instruction, while the cost of private teaching, and an acquaintance with the mysteries of knowledge, placed them within the reach of only very few individuals. The result was such as to justify the following sad though beautiful reflection of a late poet and metaphysician, who was fully competent to pronounce sentence on the history and operation of all ancient opinions : " Across the night of paganism philosophy flitted on, like the lantern-fly of the tropics, a light to itself, and an ornament ; but alas ! no more than an ornament of the surrounding darkness." [*]

Perhaps if we seek a reason why it was not more useful, it will be found in the fact that its best parts were kept secret instead of being allowed to flow

[*] "Aids to Reflection," p. 183. First edition.

out upon the mass of the people, and if possible to undermine the foundations of superstition. This is the charge brought against the more enlightened men of those times by the apostle of the Gentiles :—" When they knew God they glorified Him not as God"—did not publicly recognise Him as the only proper object of adoration; hence " they became vain in their imaginations, and their foolish hearts were darkened." The film thickened on their sight, through their unfaithfulness to truth in refusing to utter their unambiguous oracles ; and in squaring their reasonings, out of mere fear and apprehension, so as not to shock popular prejudices by a single frown on polytheism and idolatry. An open attack on these might have led to the banishment of aggressive parties, or thrown them into prison, and left them no alternative but recantation, or a cup of hemlock—sacrifices which a genuine lover of truth should be ready to make at any and every call, glorying that he was counted worthy to bear the shame for her name. They, however, found it more expedient to make provision for secret discipleship.

Christianity, on the contrary, disdained to walk in craftiness, and had therefore to look elsewhere for men who would face such an ordeal. And where did she find them ? Mending their nets, or sitting at the receipt of custom. Hitherto the world in general had seen leaves and blossoms without fruit; energy did not burst into action; the sap ceased to rise, and the vintage failed. In consequence of this the Divine husbandman selected His own labourers, and appointed them Adam's task— to till the ground, to weed out the rank growth of corruption, and to cultivate in themselves and others the germs of supreme excellence.

The doctrines as well as the precepts of the gospel were, from the first, directed to practical ends. Nothing fell from the lips of its great Author so abstract and sublime as to have no connection with the affections and duties of His servants. Unto them, therefore, was it given to "know the mysteries of the kingdom of God," because these very mysteries involved right views of truth and of moral obligation. The Holy Spirit was bestowed that they might be "able to bear" still more than the Saviour could impart to them during His earthly ministrations.* Every accession, however, to their knowledge, even respecting the ineffable peculiarities of the Christian scheme, was to stimulate them to obedience and to aid its propagation.

It was intended from the beginning that the

* John xvi. 12, 13.

gospel should fix a distinctive *character* on its adherents. The love of God, the Sonship and supremacy of the Lord Jesus, the sufferings He endured, the offices of the Spirit, etc., were not to constitute a barren transcendentalism, to be numbered among visionary speculations, but to change the heart, and to produce the most striking moral results the world had ever witnessed. That Jesus Christ came to save sinners is the declaration of the God of truth, not a theory of human invention. This is the method taken by Infinite Love to redeem guilty man. No person who believed this announcement could rest any longer in ritual formalities. He might not tell the change; he might not at once pass over, in the sight of his fellow-men, to the ranks of the Captain of salvation, but he would be under Him in spirit, nor would conscience be quiet until he pacified it by obedience. And as the Messiah and His system were novel, repulsive to Jews and Greeks, and destructive to self-righteousness, so His followers became equally peculiar and repulsive, and were reckoned "the offscouring of all things." None could compromise to avoid the offence of the cross. An immediate obligation was imposed on him to take it up, and not to lay it down till he reached the threshold of the grave.

The reader will have noticed in these observations two things, which evince the truth of the position that stands at the head of this section. The first is, that Jesus Christ did not adopt a twofold form of doctrine, the one secret, the other popular, but made the whole stream of truth the common possession of His followers. He imparted its most sublime discoveries even unto babes. The poor, the humble, and the uninstructed—infants in knowledge—were invited to the school of Christ, and soon brought surpassing honour to their Teacher, leaving the scribe, the Pharisee, and the sophist in swaddling-bands, while they grew to the stature of men. It was out of the mouths of sucklings that He perfected praise. When others turned to vain janglings, these followed the footsteps of the Lord Jesus, hung upon the lips of Eternal Wisdom, and were replenished with it from "the Light of the world." He unlocked the rarest treasures of the universe, and distributed them promiscuously, "without money and without price;" He spake as never man spake, and yet made His doctrine "distil as the dew:" He blessed all lowly minds with His Spirit, made a feast of fat things to all nations, invited them to His table, and giving His apostles the tongues of "Parthians, Medes, Elamites, and the dwellers in Mesopotamia," sent them as heralds of mercy, to proclaim to the wretched, impoverished children of men, the unsearchable riches of His salvation. They went forth under the positive injunction, " Freely ye have received, freely give," and hosts of converts crowned their ministrations. Philosophers and oracles were struck dumb, and the light they had sought to confine, broke in on the human mind from a quarter they could never darken, any more than they could spread a pall across the broad vault of heaven, and close " the eyelids of the morning " upon man.

The second thing here urged is that the doctrines of the cross involved opposition to existing doctrines, and that it was part of the scheme to engage in its own support and extension every living illustration of its power. The Saviour required self-denial of all His disciples, without attempting to conceal the dangers to which they were exposed. He did not encourage them to tread in a rough, uneven path for His sake, if, by possibility, one should present itself; but informed them beforehand that it would be their daily lot, and that the time would come when those who killed them would think they were doing God service. Christianity, therefore, not only excluded the conduct now under consideration, but such conduct was utterly incompatible with its nature, institutions, and obligations. Experimentally, we allow it was spiritual and invisible; practically, it was "the manifestation of the truth to every man's conscience in the sight of God." The followers of Christ were to renounce all selfish views, and to live only for His praise. Neither evil report nor good report was to shake their purpose. He had selected them for this work, impressed on them the principles of a new religion, constituted fishermen and publicans and sinners the teachers of mankind; and setting on them His own mark, knowing at the same time that none could mistake them, He avowedly sent them forth as "sheep among wolves." He could take no pleasure in contemplating their position in connection with its moral ends. It was in this way they were to make the gospel its own witness, and by example, as well as direct instruction, to prostrate all forms of sin and falsehood, before the majesty of holiness and truth. Has He then made any new provision for the present day? Has He in any measure changed His purpose or requisitions? Does He not allow us to accommodate the profession of Christianity to our own feelings? Or now that He has cooled the flames of persecution, does He tolerate pusillanimity, when, during their seven-fold heat, He did not tolerate fear? We are content to leave the answer to these questions with the conscience of every secret disciple. "We ought to obey God rather than man," will be its instantaneous decision. This was the apostolic motto, and it is worthy of all acceptation. The sentiment conveyed in it is not conventional but universal. It is co-extensive with all pure morality, with all that is thought duty. It is the voice of sound philosophy as well as of religion. Ancient teachers of virtue inculcate it, Jesus Christ did the same, and expects His disciples to enforce it by example. The roots of religious principle are not merely to strike into the heart and to spread beneath the surface, but to manifest their existence and their growth by the fruits of righteousness, and to beautify the earth with a holy vegetation : " The Spirit and the bride say, Come ; and *let him that heareth* say, Come," until the united voices of the saints be as the sound of many waters, whose echo shall fill our fallen world with the glad tidings of salvation.

2. *By concealing our love to Christ, we grieve and quench the Spirit of God.*—A person who loves the Lord Jesus Christ is conscious of religious sentiments more pure, varied, and powerful than the moral emotions of the best days of his unregenerate state. The contemplation of the Lamb of God softens the heart, and introduces a new order of feelings to his experience. He attributes

this change, in the views it embraces, and in the joy accompanying it, to the Holy Spirit, who graciously undertakes this part of the work of redemption. By His power, ignorance and prejudice, like mists at the break of day, vanish out of sight. A Saviour—the only yet all-sufficient hope of the penitent—is revealed in a way admirably adapted to inspire hope, gratitude, and faith. These graces bring into existence, as to the distinctive faculties of man, corresponding obligations. They are in themselves exercises of the mind, and according to its bias, and the truths and objects before it, are they called into being and operation. Love, meekness, temperance, etc., become steady by the repetition of single acts, but permanency belongs to the mind only, not to its affections. Thus trust in the adorable Redeemer may continue for a few moments, recur at devotional hours, or, in a better example, pervade the thoughts, and then sink—spiritual life being often in a state of suspended animation—into a feeble and infrequent reference to the Christian Propitiation. This view of the case, without interfering in the slightest degree with the purpose of God, or the perseverance of the saints, will evince the importance of attending to *all* the suggestions of the Holy Spirit, since inattention breaks the current of religious emotion, and prevents it from acquiring strength, depth, and amplitude sufficient to overpower and carry off the pollutions of the world. Now it is impossible for a secret disciple to regard these silent monitiors of the Spirit of truth. His practice is visible union with the world. What application can his case afford of the following criterion :— " By *this* shall all men know that ye are my disciples, *if ye have love one to another*"? Where is the spectacle? When the children of a family separate from each other, acknowledge no relation, and keep up no intercourse, the common impression is that they are mutually indifferent—*without natural affection*. It is similar as to " the household of faith." Here he who " follows afar off," induces the belief that he has no connection with the Church. His own conscience enforces the substance of this charge, and fills his solitude with lamentation :

" My fellow-Christians need help in their conflict with the great adversary, yet I stand aloof, and take no part in their operations. I give no significant expression to my love for them, which, however, I feel, and hereby know that I am 'born of God.' Jesus Christ fills my thoughts, and still I allow not the expression of the love I cherish towards Him to drop from my lips in the hearing of any human being. Moral men, who care little for Divine truth, often inculcate good principles and silence impiety; I do both of these things in some measure by my behaviour, but not as a follower of Christ, not as revering His authority, and ready at any hazard to bear witness to His name."

Such self-upbraiding is by no means uncommon with this class of individuals when they are alone. They retire from worldly society, disgusted with it the more because it has been a fresh occasion of unfaithfulness to their convictions. And the less they avowed themselves, the more they stifled the rising emotions of religion. But is not this quenching the Spirit? Is not this doing violence to those heavenly warnings which bespeak His influence upon the heart? When the blessed Redeemer gave the promise of the Holy Spirit to His apostles, he added, apparently as a consequence of His descent, " *Ye* also shall bear witness of me." Had they been insensible to His all-constraining love, or studious to conceal their views of His glory, they would so far have thwarted the very intent of that exalted bestowment. His influences were shed abroad, not merely for their good, but that they might speak and testify concerning Christ. The mission of the Son of God, His triumph over death, His session at the right hand of the Father, His propitiatory character, and His ability to save were truths too momentous for concealment. And they not only retain their original importance, but are employed by the same great Agent for the same end. *He* evinces His complacency in the Lord Jesus by setting in full view His exalted attributes, by carrying into effect the councils of eternal love, and by diffusing among mankind the knowledge of salvation. In so doing, He expects not resistance, but co-operation. He teaches us, that we may teach others "the deep things of God." Virtue comes from Him that we may be links in the chain of communication. We are to touch the springs of other minds, in order to awaken movements that accord with the further designs of justice or of mercy. In this He employs those whom He enlightens: and every Christian may easily satisfy himself that he is both grieving the Spirit, and virtually denying Christ, whenever his conduct, as a whole, does not tend to "the furtherance of the gospel." He may safely take one step more, and assure his own soul that, in spite of all the carnal conformity of some professors, it is incumbent on *him* to throw the largest amount of religious principle and feeling, into every *particular* of human life. The Holy Spirit waits for his exertions.

Abandon these strongholds of practical piety, annul this object, and there will be no duty for the Church to discharge. We shall at once withdraw the instrumentality which God has condescended to employ in the propagation of Divine truth, and leave the conversion of souls to illapses as extraordinary as those of the apostolic age. This, however, is not the Divine plan. The Spirit of God, though perfectly free and sovereign, has indicated the general line and law of His operations. The sun gives light to the moon, the Spirit to the Church, the Church to the world. He chooses not as His abode an unfrequented, solitary temple, whose interior is illumined simply for Himself; the habitation He delights in is a heart where His handiwork may be seen, reflecting through a thousand apertures the glory which emanates from His indwelling presence. Whoever, therefore, limits the truth to his own breast, robs the Holy Spirit of the honour that is due to Him, and, so far, wrests from His hand the weapon it was His intention to employ against the adversaries of the Cross. That the counsel of God will stand is true, but that He, in marvellous kindness, makes use of our energies, in proportion as we put them forth, is equally true and constitutes the joy of all who labour for the glory of His name. Thus then is that blessed Agent who renews the soul, either encouraged or repulsed according as we attend to or neglect His holy solicitations. If timid, when He exhorts us to be of good courage, if mute, when we should lift up our voice like a trumpet, if we put on disguise when we should appear on the Lord's side, nothing can prove more surely that we are conferring with flesh and blood, nothing tend more effectually to the extinction of heartfelt piety. Shall the Holy Spirit then retire until such persons acknowledge their iniquities? Shall the scene He has beautified be darkened by the withdrawal of His beams? We know of no alternative. An obstinate refusal to honour the glorious Immanuel, whom the Comforter delights to honour, *must* becloud the soul, *must* quench "joy in the Holy Ghost," and lead to that discipline which shall at length subdue the contumacious opposition of the flesh, and rescue the spirit from final condemnation in the day of the Lord Jesus. We deny not that the subjects of this infirmity may be saved; but after the repeated checks they have put upon the growth of religion, the ascendancy which Satan has had in all their counsels, the opportunities afforded him of sapping the foundations of all holiness, they will not only "scarcely be saved," but, at last, saved "so as by fire."

3. *The avowal of our faith, and the exemplification of our principles, may have a moral influence on others.*—Man is susceptible of impressions, painful or pleasing, good or evil, according to the objects around him. When shut out from the sight of virtue, and reared amid scenes of sin, there is little hope, save under a change of discipline, of his moral regeneration. Ordinary circumstances, however, afford various means of arousing conscience into life and power. The consequences of crime, the solemnity of death, the example of good men, the pleasures of religion, may each and all be touched with effect, as occasion serves, by any person of simple piety and moderate discrimination. At the same time it is matter of joy that conversational aptness is not essential to teach the best lessons that mankind can learn. The Saviour, in the following passage, has pointed out a more excellent way :—" Let your light so shine before men that they may see your good works, and glorify your Father which is in heaven." Men may cavil at argument, and be deaf to entreaty, but they cannot so easily either question, mistake, or resist " the finger of God," when He traces His own image in the conduct of His servants, " not in tables of stone, but in fleshly tables of the heart."

Leighton, by the purity of his life, turned a wealthy merchant from the continual accumulation of money to the nobler study of laying up treasure in heaven. It is in this manner that one human being acts upon another. There is a mirror in the mind which will always reflect the features of marked and decided piety. Students at college have been known thus to blunt the shafts of ridicule, and to draw those who once indulged in scorn to delight in prayer and praise. Sons and daughters who, by an affecting inversion of moral order, have, like the publicans and sinners of former days, entered into the kingdom of God before their parents, have yet induced these to attend the sanctuary to their salvation. Ministers and friends, when they wish to inculcate early piety, are glad to have some instance to hold up as worthy of imitation. On all hands and in every way, the power of example is illustrated, recognised, and confessed. But secret disciples virtually abrogate this law, and violate all the analogies of social life. Here the exhibition, profession, and inculcation of honesty, kindness, truth, etc., are rightly judged the proper means of amending the heart, and making virtue descend to posterity. And in the same way must we nurture the principles of religion if we are at all desirous of witnessing their operation. Suppose, for instance, a father or mother to make no positive confession of the care of Providence, can they expect their children to retain God in their knowledge? Or if they recognise His general goodness, and attend His courts, without discarding worldly habits, and become one with the Church of Christ, praying for their offspring, and teaching them the doctrines of salvation, can they anticipate, on any reasonable ground, the results of parental piety?—" Do men gather grapes of thorns, or figs of thistles?"

Similar observations are applicable to a wider circle. The moral influence we exert over our acquaintance depends upon their knowledge of our principles. It is not enough that they witness a correct behaviour, and a regular discharge of the relative duties of life; we must be "epistles of Christ, known and read of all men." This is not the case with the secret disciple. Even the motives he assigns for virtue are beneath the gospel, and his moral excellence itself is derived from a source which he is unwilling to confess. His character has the effect of equivocation. He does not deny Christ; he does not avow Him. It is not even possible, except on rare occasions, when there are certain slips of Christian sentiment, to identify him as the Jews did Peter—" Thou also art one of them, for thy *speech* bewrayeth thee."

We acknowledge it a higher aim to *be* good than to appear so, but the blessed Saviour united the two, and He is our pattern. An individual who hides his real sentiments may be admired by others as of an excellent disposition, but this detracts immeasurably from the force of his example as the effect of Divine grace. It puts a restraint, often found necessary, on the spontaneous tendencies, and the full illustration, of practical Christianity. Nor is this the whole of the evil. A feeling that he is not irrevocably pledged to a religious course arises, on infernal suggestion, to help him at each new stretch of conscience that is called for by the peculiarities of his situation. As he refuses to draw a line beyond which he will not go, his friends are aware of no violence in taking him with them into unholy associations. A direct negative, therefore is put on all the thoughts, acts, counsels, and habits of the Christian, *as such*, since he conforms to the world, and, on many occasions, enters into a questionable alliance with the elements of impiety. He bows in the house of Rimmon without apprising the worshippers that his is an unwilling compliance with civil forms, not an act of genuine idolatry.

The respectability of character attached usually to this class, combined with reserve and indecision as to the chief good, has, we allow, a tendency to impress on others its own likeness. But the great matter of lamentation is, that it is only the exterior that transfers itself; not the love, faith, penitence, and sacred aspirations of the heart. It is these we want to make "manifest in the flesh." This is the force we wish brought into the field.

Let such persons avow their obligations to the Saviour of sinners, and they will be at once identified with His cause. It will lead them to family devotion, to speak of the ministry they attend, to spread missionary information, to expostulate with ungodly connections, to act in all things as the servants of Christ, whose motto is, "Doing the will of God from the heart."

The reader must be sensible of the very different impressions this is likely to produce on other minds. Here thought is embodied in action, and substance is given to the shadowy outlines and spiritualities of "the highest style of man." Howard, as a secret philanthropist, even admitting he had done much, would never have acquired the power which now belongs to his name. But he told his tale, declared his purpose, and acted on it; what he did men felt, and though he is dead, his very statue pleads for the wretched, and prevails. All the forms of being that existed in the

Divine mind before the six days, had no effect on "the sons of God" until thrown into creation; then they "shouted for joy." The emotions and reflections which a Christian may command, depend on a similar manifestation. A profession of faith, sustained by piety, may arrest attention, and, in this simple operation, stand at the head of a train of agents, which, when fairly brought on, shall work mightily in the regeneration of the soul. This is an instrumentality which the Divine Spirit often employs in the conversion of men. And while we regard it only in the common light of moral causation, it is to be remembered that we are not at liberty to set aside the laws of the human mind. Secret discipleship fails, as to God and man, in submission to the one, in adaptation to the other. It recognises no external relation, slights the example of Christ, gives no attestation to the truth. We may therefore regard it as abrogating several of the leading duties of Christianity, and leaving us no alternative but to admonish those who adopt it, by the allegiance they owe their Master, to come out and be separate. The benefit they may confer on their fellow-creatures, the moral influence that may operate slowly, though surely, on those around them, should be an encouragement to the course we recommend.

Time melts into eternity; the present affects the whole of the future, and happy is he who contributes in the smallest measure to "save a soul from death, and to hide a multitude of sins."

4. *Jesus Christ is worthy of being confessed before all intelligent creatures.*—The sentiments of good men merit at all times candid consideration. A moralist will not think lightly of any affection which has had the sanction of the virtuous of all ages. And most of the rules that are important in ethics are important in religion. What then has been the uniform practice of pious minds with respect to Jesus Christ? Have they not spoken of Him in terms which, if true, render Him the object worthy of universal admiration? Have they not delighted to dwell on His name as "the Alpha and Omega, the beginning and end" of all things? Whence did they derive this practice? If we follow the windings of a stream we shall at last reach its source. The apostles spake, undoubtedly, as they were moved by the Holy Spirit. Ultimately, therefore, the ascriptions given to Christ must be attributed to direct inspiration. Thence they were adopted by the Church. The most distinguished saints of every age have proclaimed His praise, and avowed their obligations.

to His love : "Of His fulness have all we received, and grace for grace."

The silent, unseen current of feeling in the soul of a secret disciple runs in the same direction. *He*, likewise, celebrates the glory of the Lord Jesus in the songs of the sanctuary, and responds to the acclamations of the spirits of just men made perfect—"Worthy is the Lamb that was slain." In this, however, he only aids the general voice, and escapes whatever is distinctive and special by mixing with the crowd. Elsewhere he has nothing to say. The same thoughts pass through his mind, but he gives them no expression. They bloom and die in their native solitudes. But why be ashamed of Jesus Christ? Is He not "the bread of life," "the light of the world," "the foundation God hath laid in Zion"? Is He not "the first and the last," "the head of the Church," "the image of the invisible God"? "Doubtless He is all these," will be the reply. And does not this reply show that it would be less culpable to "muffle up" the sun than it is to veil the excellences of Christ from the eyes of man? Is not virtue the dignity of man? Can we dispense with a single example of its power? And if not, how can we, with the *standard* and *model* of goodness itself? The absolute is the ground of the comparative ; the perfect the criterion of the imperfect.

The Saviour commands us to confess His name, and He has the most equitable claim to our obedience and love, both from the exclusive prerogatives of His office, and the perfection of His nature. He is King in Zion. An earthly prince may have just authority, and employ it in advancing the prosperity of his people, while his personal character may be by no means worthy or exalted. We therefore usually regard the public measures, not the private conduct, of ruling powers. But when we meet, as in an Alfred, with the combination of the two, there is then every attraction in dignity, every quality that can satisfy a nation, every grace that can ornament a throne. It is gratifying to find this rare and admirable union where it is likely to be most influential, not only in petty principalities, but reflected upon them from a Power confessedly supreme. This is a sublime order, which, like the sun amid the planetary system, concentrates the greatest light and glory, where they ought most conspicuously to shine.

Now this is the case with the Lord Jesus Christ. He is so high, that all the angels of God worship Him; so holy, that He is without blemish; so comprehensive in His wisdom, that in Him are all its treasures; so benignant, that He extends mercy to His foes; so powerful, that He can melt "the heart of stone;" exempt from defect by a fulness of natural and moral attributes;—His character altogether lovely, His dignity higher than the heavens. There is no exaggeration in this statement, it is taken from the Scriptures of truth. And if so, is not the only Mediator between God and man worthy of universal acknowledgment? What is the declared purpose of His exaltation? "That at the name of Jesus every knee should bow, of things in heaven, and things in earth, and things under the earth; and that every tongue should confess that Jesus Christ is Lord, to the glory of God the Father." "The Father loveth the Son, and hath committed all things into His hands, that all men should honour the Son, even as they honour the Father. He that honoureth not the Son, honoureth not the Father who sent Him."

That which we are assured is pleasing to God should become the pleasure of His creatures. A pious naturalist will examine the fossil remains of ancient times, and the exquisite forms of animate and inanimate existence, in order to gather from the records of creation a theology which, as far as it goes, shall bring some humble tribute of praise to the footstool of Omnipotence. The usual sentiments of the Christian church, drawn from revealed truth, do Him higher homage as the God of salvation. We account it a becoming exercise to adore Him as the " Father of mercies," the " God of the spirits of all flesh." But this united praise, to be acceptable, must have special reference to *Him* by whom all things consist. The Father has entrusted the visible administration of heaven and earth to the Lord Jesus, that like acknowledgments may be made to Him " who is, who was, and who is to come, the Almighty."

There are also other respects in which the Author of eternal salvation merits public and devout recognition on the part of all His followers. His sufferings evinced the purest benevolence, and were endured to redeem man ; ours never can possess a propitiatory quality, and must issue in personal advantage. We reap the harvest of *His* toil. Bowed down with a weight of guilt which we could not remove, it was not possible for us to look up to heaven with hope, nor forward to eternity with satisfaction. The best blessings were beyond our reach ; now they are put into our hands. The poverty of Lazarus is no bar to boundless wealth ; the weakest pinions that could not rise above the earth, may now plume their flight for the third heavens.

Are, then, pardon and peace and immortality—all the inestimable fruits of atoning love—to be received in silence, while we speak aloud of the common mercies of the day? Are we to be mute respecting the *grace* of God, that peculiar measure of His government, which is to people heaven by redeeming the inhabitants of a lost district of creation? We look for the expression of joy when the doors of a dungeon are thrown open, and the voice of authority proclaims deliverance to the captive; and equally natural is it to expect that the abundance of the heart will overflow when self-convicted sinners hear that there is salvation in the Cross.

No ordinary being can forgive sin; it is the prerogative of God. And as the reason of it is found in Christ, extending still farther in the moral renovation, the happiness and immortality of the soul, these are consequences so sublime and momentous as to merit all manner of notoriety and notice. But how are they to be known, if believers substitute secrecy for "the manifestation of the truth"? If *they* practically consign the glories of Christ to oblivion, who, in our world, is to give them publicity? The excellences of the Saviour are the foundation of all our hopes. The endless enjoyment of Divine favour must include all possible good, and whoever confers on us this good must occupy the highest pinnacle of visible or conceivable authority. We attach utility and even greatness to a power which contemplates extensive social and political improvements. The increase of happiness resulting not only to present but future generations, is grateful to human feelings; and the mind which plans it, and gathers together the energies for carrying it into effect, possesses, in our esteem, a glory commensurate with the ample range he has chosen in which to display his powers of beneficence. Should he contemplate a strictly moral object—the annihilation of intemperance—an effective system of religious education for millions of youth successively coming under it to the end of time—the more unclouded our judgments, the more pure our minds, the greater would be the complacence we should feel in this above the former object, as one that would outwit and immeasurably surpass the wisest expedients of the most sagacious and mighty politicians. But multiply the benefits to the end of the world by all the myriads that might be benefited, and one soul in the possession of eternal life would have within itself the power of exhausting the entire good of the species, *limited to time,* until it would all fade from sight as the minor variations of the earth to the beings that soar among the stars. The bestowment of eternal blessedness on the guilty is a boon worthy of the infinite liberality of His hand, who in all things is to have the pre-eminence. Hyperbole here is impossible, and were the universe collected together to witness this vouchsafement to a single sinner, it would be only a fit assemblage for such a spectacle. Yet this unutterable good will not be limited to a few. The blood of Christ will cleanse the innumerable host which was presented in vision to the apostle John, as standing before the throne, and crying with a loud voice, "Salvation to our God who sitteth upon the throne, and unto the Lamb." Where, then, we ask the secret disciple, is your gratitude to the Saviour of sinners? You have been favoured with a spiritual insight to Divine truth, and under conscious vileness and guilt, led to make the inquiry, "What shall I do to be saved?" This brought you to Christ. The New Testament made you acquainted with His dignity, and it was—perhaps is now—to you a wonderful fact, that the Son of God should veil His glory, by the assumption of our nature, and die on the cross as the propitiation for our sins. His history possessed for you every charm, and at each step you paused to admire some new display of His marvellous character and matchless grace,

The ingratitude, hatred, persecution, and reproaches of those whom He came to redeem, served only to place in a stronger light the benevolence, love, long-suffering, and fortitude of the Saviour. You were often struck with amazement at the unshaken steadfastness with which He was intent on doing good to man, when man was spurning the proffers of His mercy, and at beholding Him quite undisturbed as to His grand object, whatever endurance it might demand, when He could have swept away every enemy in an instant to perdition. You followed Him to the cross, and seeming to hear again the prayer, " Father, forgive them," your admiration was complete ; you dwelt on the consummation of greatness itself, and associated with the whole the extensive benefits that would flow to man, and the hope and prospect of your own personal redemption. Your feelings then, and in all like moments, were those of intense, grateful affection. Has, then, Christ ceased His active interest on your behalf? Is He less to you than He was? Are His merits and intercession less needful for your acceptance and justification? Were your emotions then wrong or too ardent? Were they extravagant when compared with the love and greatness and grace to which they were directed? Not a word of this will you dare to utter. Let us, then, contrast the conduct of Christ with yours. He endured the contradiction of sinners for your sake, you are unwilling to participate in the reproach: he foresaw all His sufferings, yet encountered them; you shrink from evils which may never happen: He made Himself a spectacle unto the world, to angels, and to men; you will not be a spectacle to either at the table of His love: He took the cup which His Father assigned Him, and drank it to the dregs; you will not take the cup which commemorates His death, and is at once the emblem of life and the earnest of salvation: He shrouded His glory beneath the ignominy of the cross; you, though you know it, refuse to exclaim, "Surely this was the Son of God!" He laid down His life that He might obtain life for you, and you virtually say, "I know not the Man."

How long shall things continue in this state? We hope well of you, it is true, believing that the day of severe trial will evince your principles. The embers that look grey and dusky often hide a deal of fire, ready at the first stirring to show itself, and, if fuel be added, to set it on a flame. It is thus, we trust, with you; but we are "jealous over you with a godly jealousy." Christ has risen, and His followers should walk in newness of life. The cries of the Church militant pierce heaven; the ark of God is in the hands of the Philistines; the world groans beneath its crimes; sinners are sinking to perdition; the blood of Christ retains its virtue; He pleads your cause in the presence of His Father; angels, and the spirits of the just adore Him; earth and heaven reproach your silence,— one by its miseries, the other by its praises; and the united goodness of both worlds implore your aid in the establishment of the kingdom of Christ, and in the celebration of His praise.

5. *The neglect of Divine ordinances grows on those who indulge it, until the habit becomes fixed, and almost invincible.*—The constant hope of secret disciples is, that it will not be long ere they avow themselves on the Lord's side. They have no intention of standing aloof from the Church all their lives. Nothing can be farther from their thoughts; nothing to them appears more remote from probability. And yet all ministers who have yearned over the spiritual well-being of their charge, will be at no loss to narrate instances in which the same false shame, the same excuses, and the same state of mind, have been perpetuated for years, until they have superinduced habitual distance and separation from the table of the Lord, and from the more distinctive characteristics of His servants. Perhaps, at the earlier stage of religious impression,

there was a disposition to linger in the sanctuary during the commemoration of the love of Christ. When the expressive rite was over, they mused silently on the privilege of believers, and the fellowship of the saints, as a happy preparation for " the marriage supper of the Lamb." They continued to frequent the house of God, and to wish themselves in the Church, until their thoughts, feelings, and wishes became fainter, and they could withdraw without misgiving or compunction, no sensible solemnity resting on their minds, and none of the features of this holy spectacle interesting their hearts and imaginations, as was the case in better days, when they loved to think of it, " sitting in the house and walking by the way."

Perhaps in no one example of this character was there, during the successive steps of declension, any apprehension of such an issue. Some false hope was ever and anon assuring the mind, checking that diligent search which a vigilant Christian will often institute into the state of the affections, and removing the great crisis of solemn dedication to God and to His Church only to a short distance in advance, that the deluded soul might seem to be approaching its object while receding from it, and might imagine itself the care of ministering spirits while the sport of " the prince of the power of the air." And yet the subject of this delusion is, by deferring the consecration of his heart to God, arraying the strongest principles of his nature against the public claims of piety and truth. Single acts in their collective force form habits. They are the links of the chains which men forge for their own bondage. An individual who is irregular in devotion, in household duties, in study, in business, etc., finds it more difficult to be decided and systematic the older he grows, and the less he restrains unsteadiness and vacillation. Religion suffers more under this law than the common interests of life. These prompt by present wants, and so far there is a counteracting agency, occasioning the rebound of the mind to its original position, while in neglecting the commands and ordinances of Christ, conscience becomes less tender, truth less impressive, piety less a life than a form, till at length indifference settles on the soul, with fixed motionless look, like a statue on a tomb. The mind then, perhaps—at this palpable distance from vital godliness—becomes just conscious of the strange stupor that has seized it. That ominous decay of sensibility, which betokened a wasting of the general powers of life, passed without notice. This more marked change is attended by a vague and misty something that tells the man his faculties are gone. Possibly no material alteration takes places in his doctrinal views or moral principles; but there is a state of apathy that the scene of Gethsemane would fail to move. He has lost that sense of moral beauty which he once saw encircling the Son of God, and no longer do his sympathies act as springs to his thoughts, so as to throw a potent spell over all holy things. A right-minded Christian will feel this to be a real calamity. Were men merely intellectual, thought would be cold and without a soul; nature would lose that ethereal presence which poetry invokes, though it is her own Divine creation; fancy would die; loveliness and sublimity be settled by a scale of magnitudes; the eye lack lustre, the face smiles, and the heart no more feel pity for the poor. The susceptibilities of man are, in relation to society and religion, the most important elements of the human constitution. When hallowed by devotion, and under enlightened control, they suggest the best deeds, and stand ready to perform them. The practice of animating religious services by hymns of praise springs from this source; and when the psalmist exclaims, "How *amiable* are thy tabernacles, O Lord of hosts!" he supplies an instance of this class of sentiments—a class that has its origin in the emotions of the heart. These act on the more refined and elevated perceptions of the mind, and, while *it* continues in a healthy state, invest with delightful attactions the life, the law, and the institutions of Christ, and spread enchantment over the whole region of piety. He who has lost these feelings has lost the "goodly pearl," and, though he retain the casket of orthodoxy, all that is made precious is no more.

There is an adaptation in the means of grace to the social affections, as well as the higher faculties of man. Preaching, prayer, communion, meditation, praise; all these nurture the vitality to which we refer, by operating on the sensibilities and imagination of the worshipper. Emotion imparts warmth to the light of reason, and without it the sublimest truths would be powerless, unfruitful speculations. And it is into this precise state of mind that the unhappy being often falls who neglects the obligations of the Christian profession. He finds himself less uneasy when he is not too strict in the duties of personal religion. It would be just the reverse had he given himself wholly to God, but, not having so done, the more devout he is, the more pungent are the stings of conscience, and the less is he able to keep at a distance from the Church. There are numerous duties which cannot be performed in secret discipleship, and he must therefore forget them, or sacrifice his peace. As he is not willing to confess Christ, this predisposes him to palliate in his own mind the criminality of disobedience. At last neglect becomes habitual, convictions have no power, and he stands in the sanctuary, when he visits it, as one of Ezekiel's slain, whom God had re-animated, and then, in judgment, extinguished the breath of life, and thrown him, a withering skeleton, back into the valley of dry bones. Then comes the "impossibility"—that is, the extreme difficulty—of "renewing him again unto repentance." He applies this passage to himself, and what has perplexed systematic theologians is perfectly easy to his apprehension. His feelings, alas, shed light upon the text! They satisfy him that it is next to impossible—for which condition we often make the expression absolute—to re-kindle the extinct fires of devotion. He knows that food is essential to life, and yet has no appetite to take it. The keen relish of truth is gone; adoption, sanctification, and redemption, are to him doctrines, and no more—without either test, evidence, or illustration in his experience. They belong, it is true, to the vitals of Christianity, but he looks at them as the anatomist at the heart and lungs after they have ceased to discharge their functions. They are parts of the system, and that is all. The reader will, perhaps, pardon me for mentioning an instance of this nature. I once addressed a young man on the subject of religion, and, not being aware of his state of mind, thought it needful to make a rapid glance at the evidences and discoveries of revelation. He, however, interrupted me, and said, "I am acquainted with all these things beforehand. My father is a clergyman. I once attended Dr. R——, a popular preacher of the present day, and went far towards making a profession of religion. It was then my delight; but I fell into gay associations, and took to reading Byron, and became another man. *I have now no feeling.* These truths affect you, but they move me no more than they do the floor on which you stand." With this he drew "Don Juan" from his breast, threw it on the ground, and looking fiercely, cursed it as it fell.

I forget the name of this gentleman, but should the above reference ever meet his eye, he will remember the spot where he made to me the painful disclosure of his state, as well as the advice and encouragement I addressed to him on that and subsequent occasions. Many secret disciples have sunk to the same depths, and then grown sensible of their wretchedness. Neglecting

Divine influence and Divine ordinances, feeling themselves at liberty to associate, settle, and act, unshackled by the consistency and discipline of a Christian Church, they have in the end been left to fix on the precincts of Sodom for their home, and almost to identify themselves with the general corruption. This, however, revolted their better principles, and, acting like an electric shock, revived some sense of energies, purity, and joy, that once were felt, and were lost only by wilful infatuation. The terrors of God then made them afraid; they passed the rest of their days in weakness, doubt, and distress; and died merely asking for mercy, instead of possessing a good hope through grace, and rejoicing in the prospect of immortality. We predict not these consequences of all who take part with them, but our solemn conviction is, that they are going the way to check all growth in grace, and to attain the sad, unenviable distinction of being able to look with invincible apathy on all religious ordinances and obligations.

6. *Conclusion.*—The pleas of the secret disciple have now been examined, and several reasons and encouragements to an avowal of his faith offered to his consideration. Let them be weighed in a fair balance. Either the Saviour is unreasonable

in demanding the open recognition of His claims, or all apologies for the opposite conduct must fall to the ground. If no justification be attempted on the part of those who slight His commands, they should at least reflect on the dangers of their situation. "Whosoever hath, to him shall be given, and he shall have more abundance; but whosoever hath not"—neglects the improvement of that he has—"from him shall be taken away even that he hath."

Admitting the defects of Christian societies, what better company will be found on earth? There Jesus Christ manifests Himself to His disciples, and where else is He so devoutly adored? You are bound to unite yourself with the family of which He is the head, to place yourself in those circumstances which will best secure your spirituality, and afford the widest scope for useful exertion. You can meet these conditions only by the renunciation of all carnal policy, the absolute surrender of yourself to Christ, and a full compliance with His injunctions. Your conduct hitherto has had a tendency to supersede His institutions. The neglect of one duty affects the discharge of another. He who can forego the communion of saints will very soon be able to resign communion with God. Instead, therefore, of pursuing the best ends, you are verging towards the worst. An immediate change in your habits is necessary. Your position is unsteady, your direction doubtful, and nothing good can follow from either. The disturbing forces around you will operate fatally on your progress, unless you at once clear them, and pursue your course. It is equally foolish and rash to hope for safety when idling within the attraction of a whirlpool.

If you wish to do good while you live, why thwart a desire so noble? The most decided exhibition of Christian principle is the best means of benefiting mankind. Every expedient that ingenuity and benevolence can devise for meliorating the condition of man is found in the Church. You may here select your department and ally yourself to fellow-labourers of like mind, who will be glad to aid and remedy individual feebleness by general combination.

If you tremble at responsibility, and quake for fear, remember that God is omnipotent. "In the Lord Jehovah is everlasting strength." There are promises of support to all who wait on Him. Jesus Christ will not disregard your prayers in the hour of temptation. His grace will be sufficient for you, and you will find that in keeping His commands there is great reward. At present you voluntarily expose yourself to the shafts of Satan; then you will be beneath the shield of the Captain of salvation. By constant humility, and by cultivating a devotional habit, you will be kept faithful unto death. Dedicate yourself, therefore, afresh to God, and yield the faculties with which He has graciously endowed you henceforth and for ever to His cause. The day of your redemption is at hand. "Yet a little while, and He that shall come will come, and will not tarry." The shadows of mortality will soon break away, and an exchange of worlds will introduce you to a scene altogether new, where the redeemed will live with Christ, and the sorrows of time will be lost in the blessedness of eternity. "The Lamb that is in the midst of the throne shall feed them, and shall lead them to living fountains of waters; and God shall wipe away all tears from their eyes."

www.ingramcontent.com/pod-product-compliance
Lightning Source LLC
Chambersburg PA
CBHW022143090426
42742CB00010B/1376